# The Mappeople
## by
# Dan Milnor

Published by Impassion Press
September 5, 2015

## FORWARD

The idea of the MAPPEOPLE came to me purely by accident one day while sketching. I was drawing a woman's hair, wondering once again-in my surrealist mind-what to do with it: set it ablaze, make it into a cloud formation or a pit of snakes. Suddenly I noticed that my meandering pencil had made what looked like a coastline....and the world of the MAPPEOPLE was born.
-D.M.


This book is dedicated to the three Greek Gods: Eros, Hypnos and Morpheus.

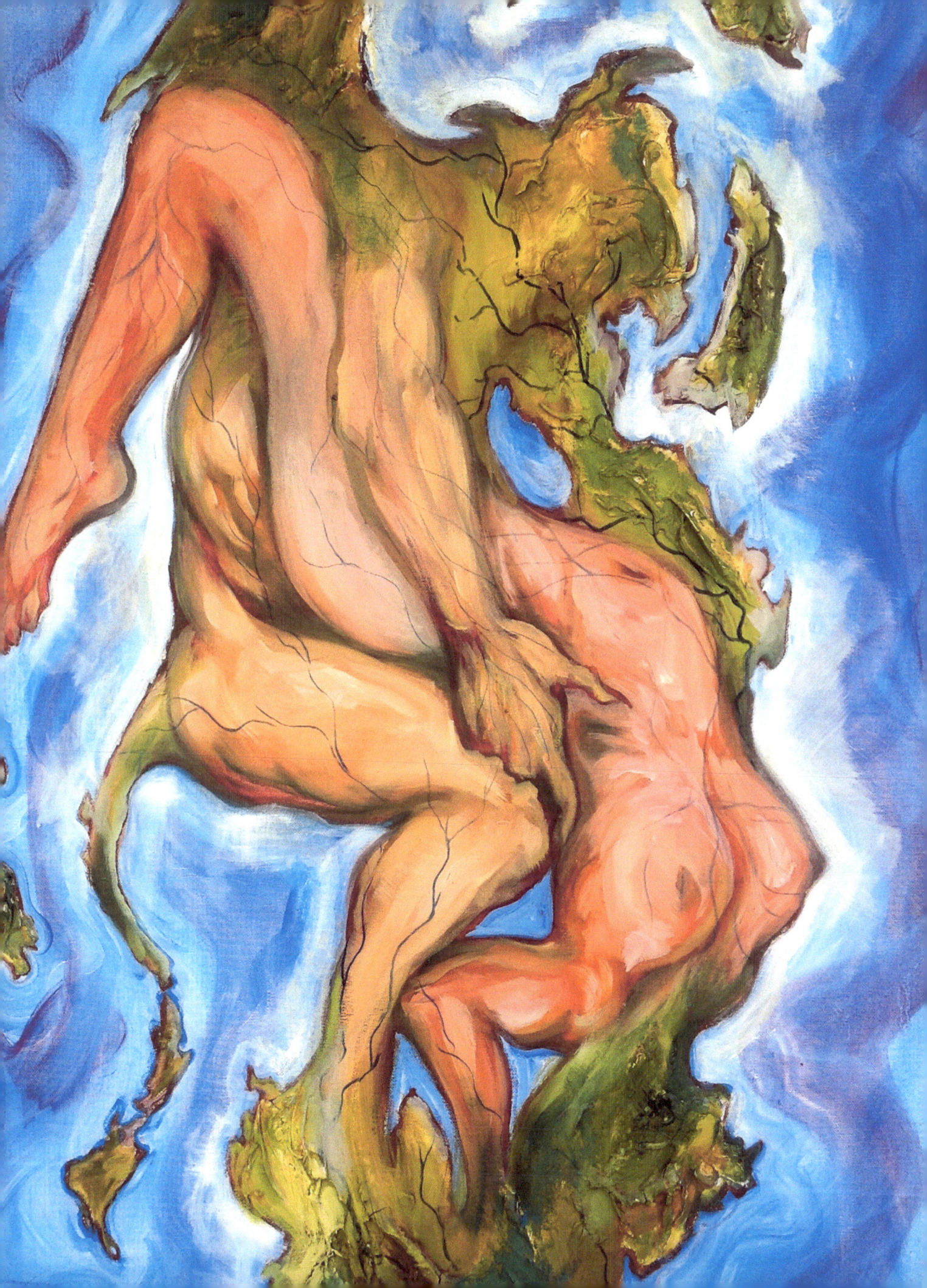

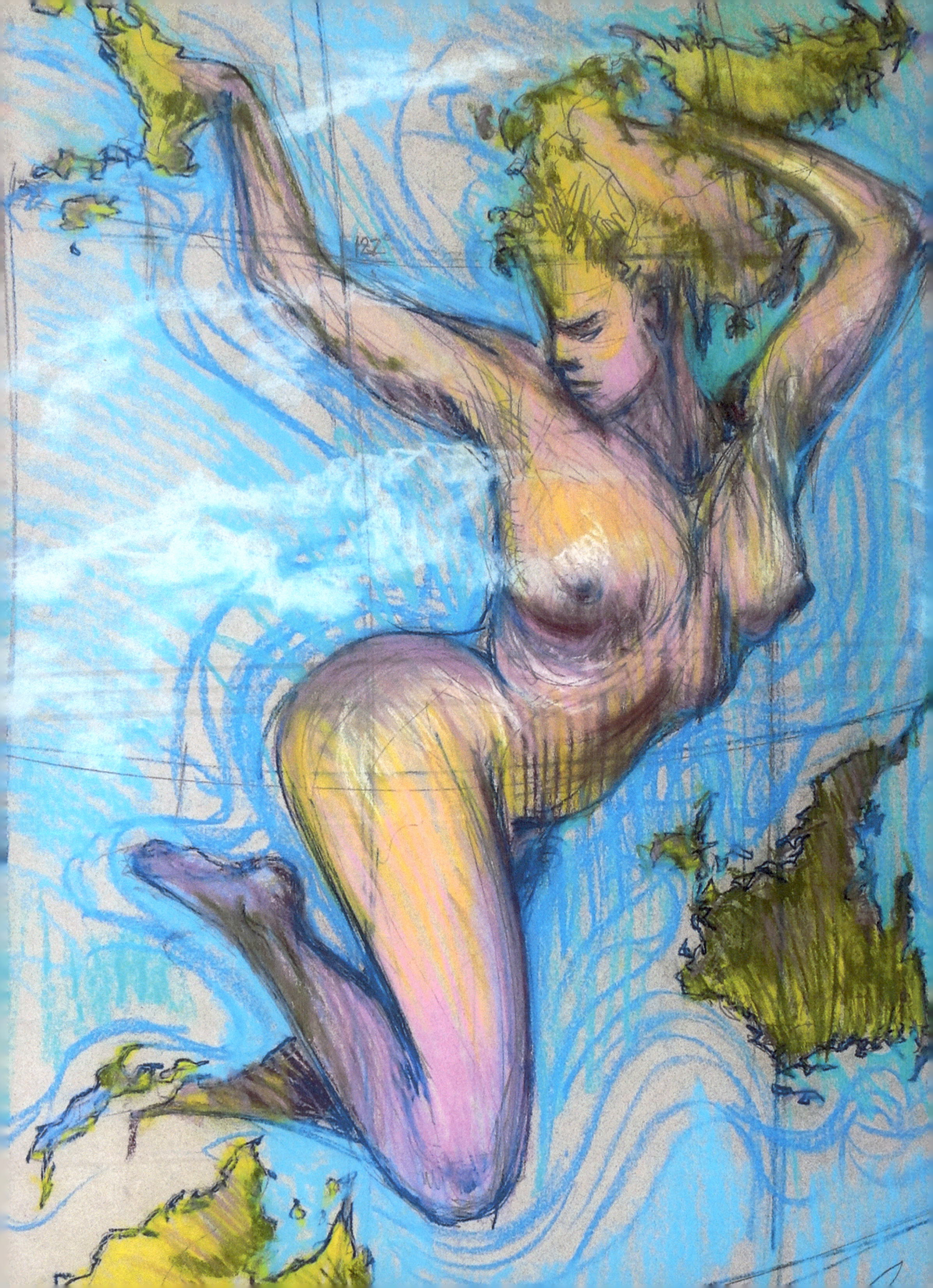

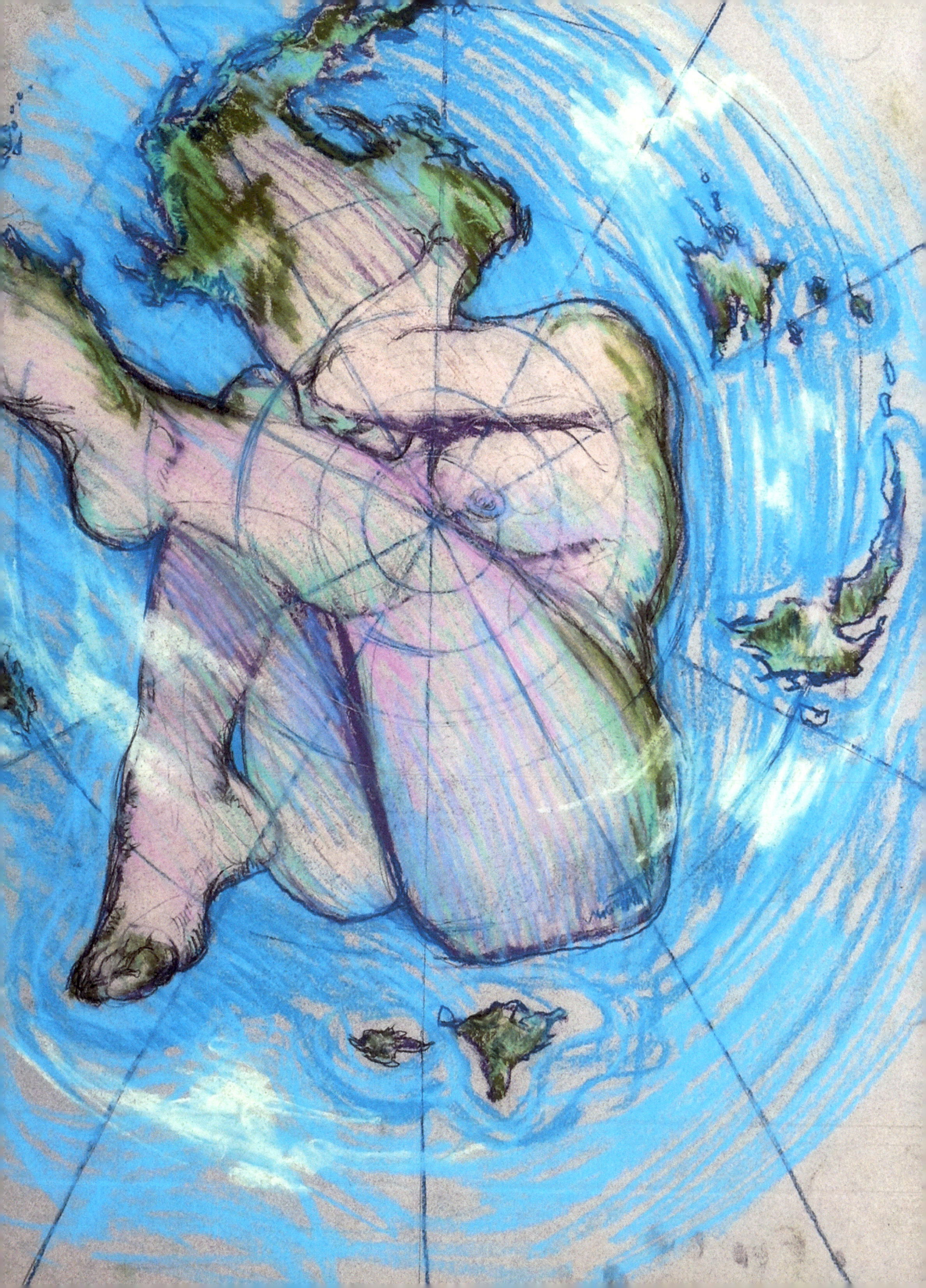

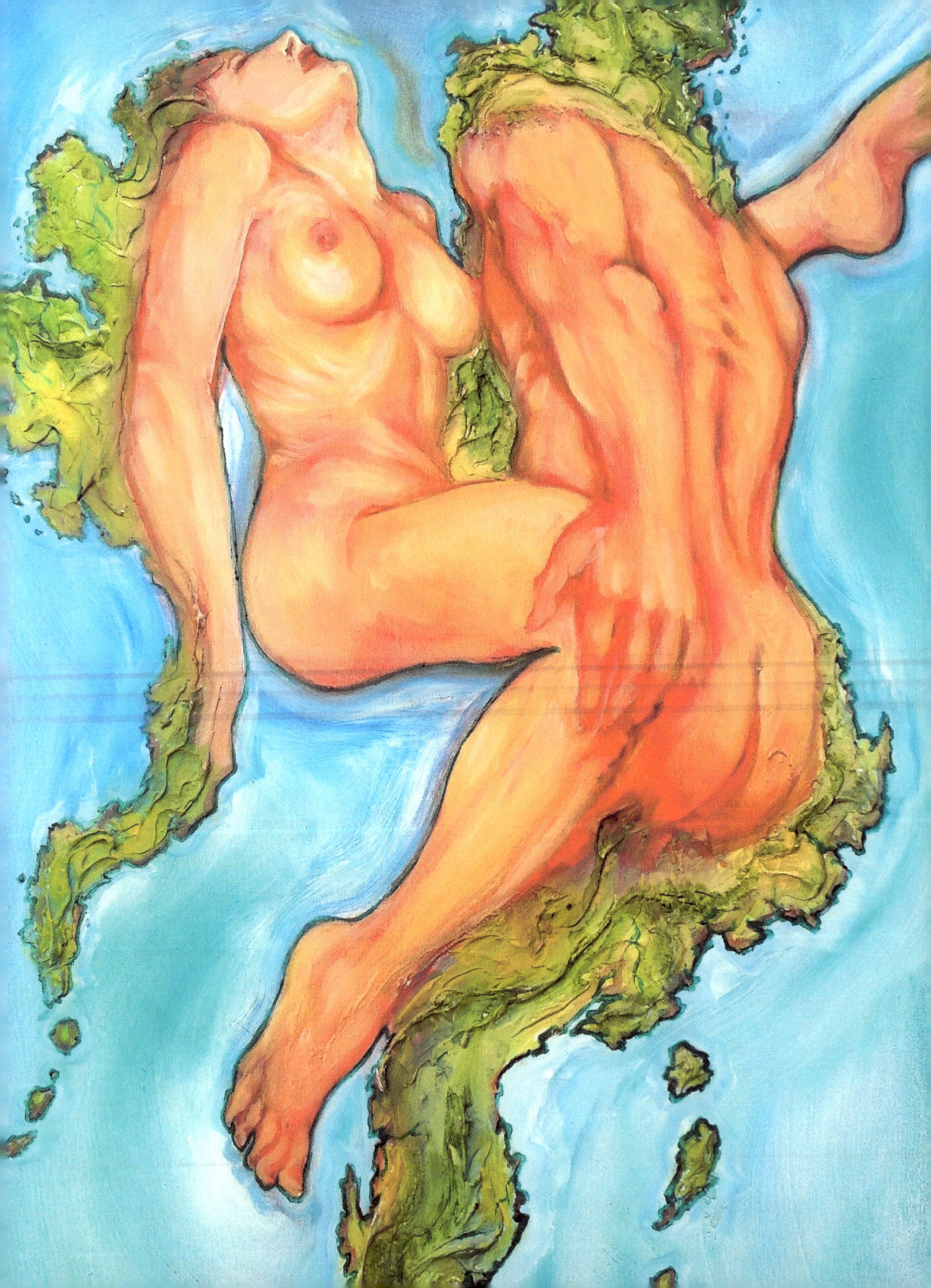

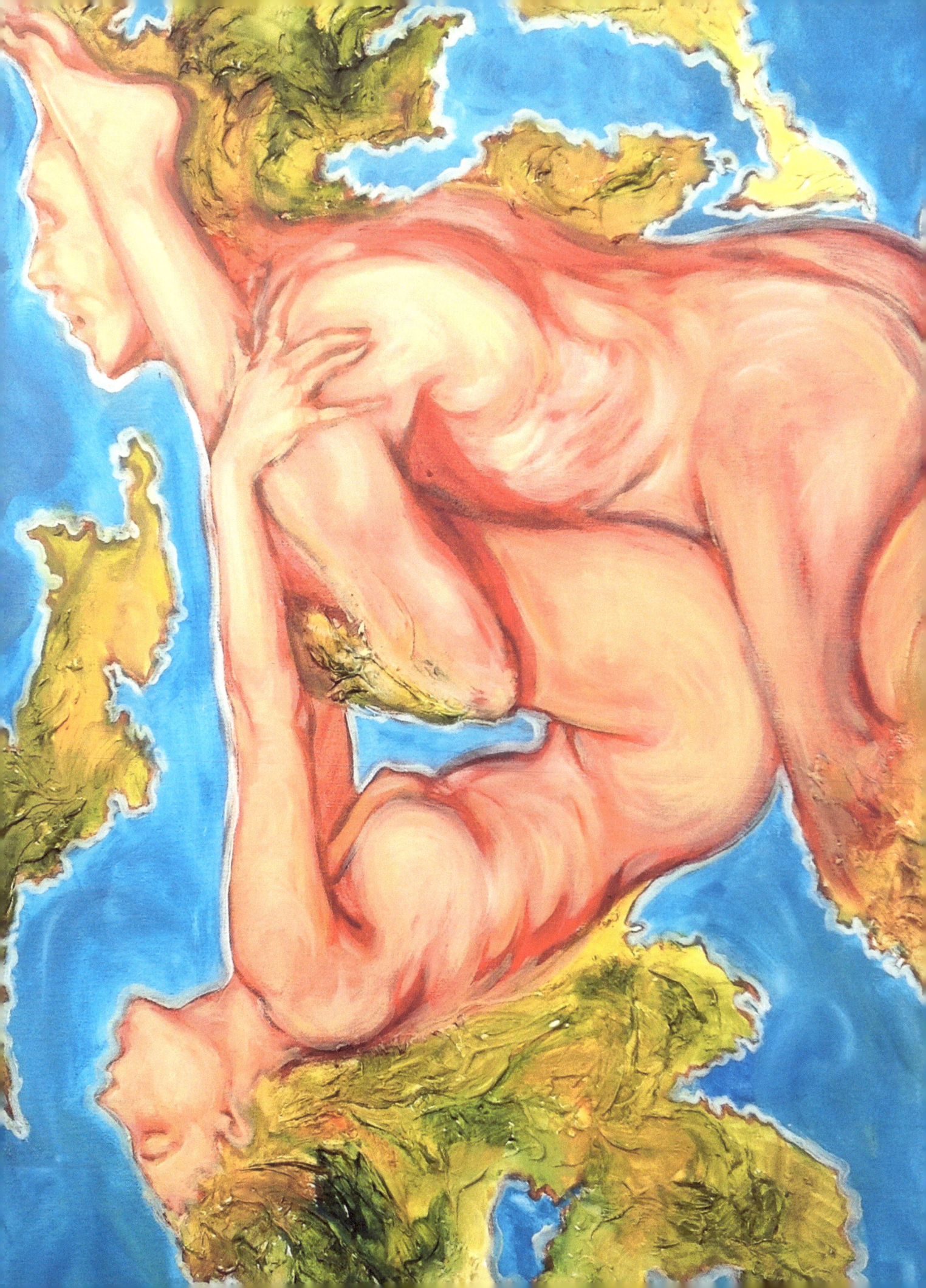

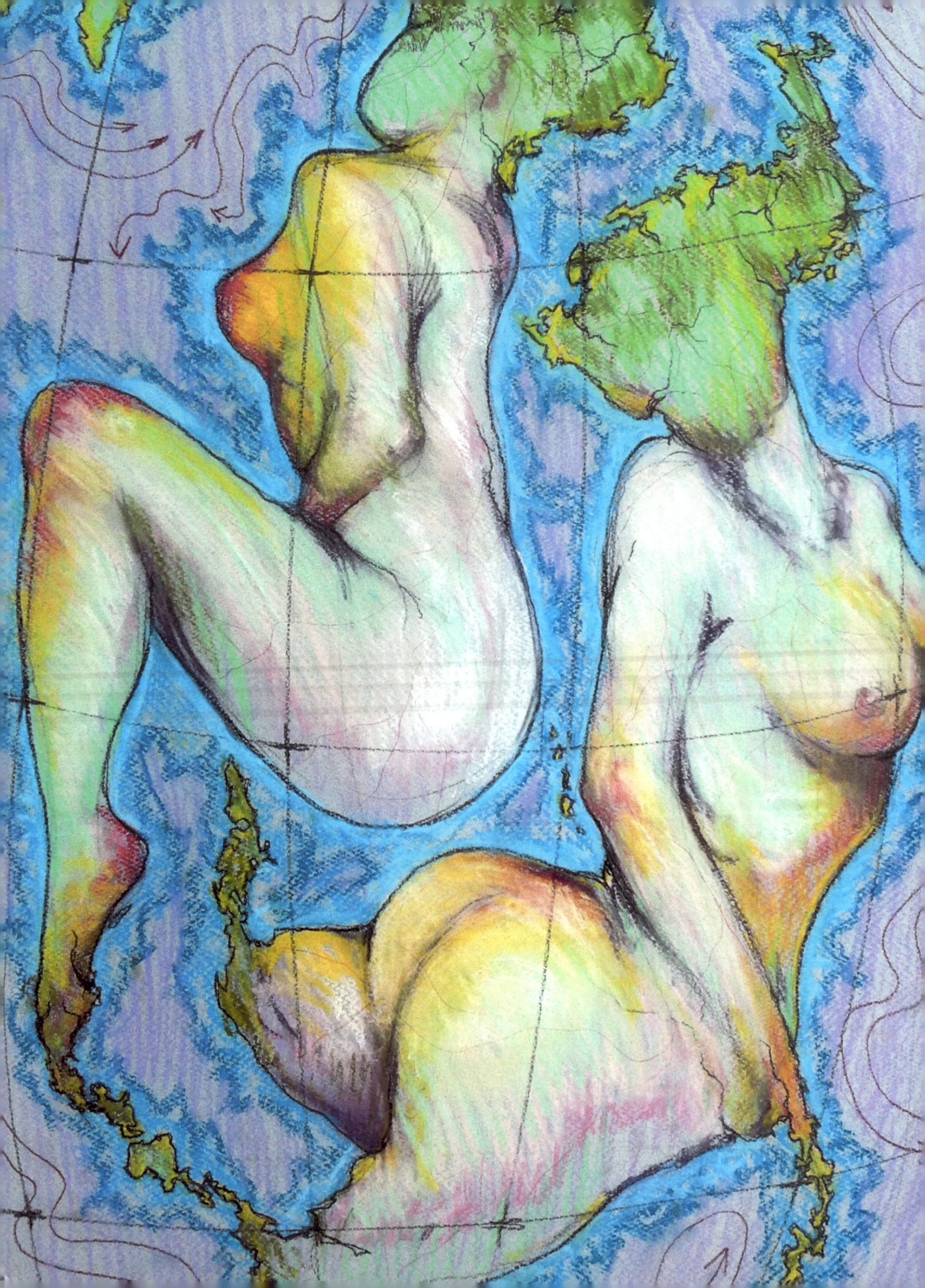

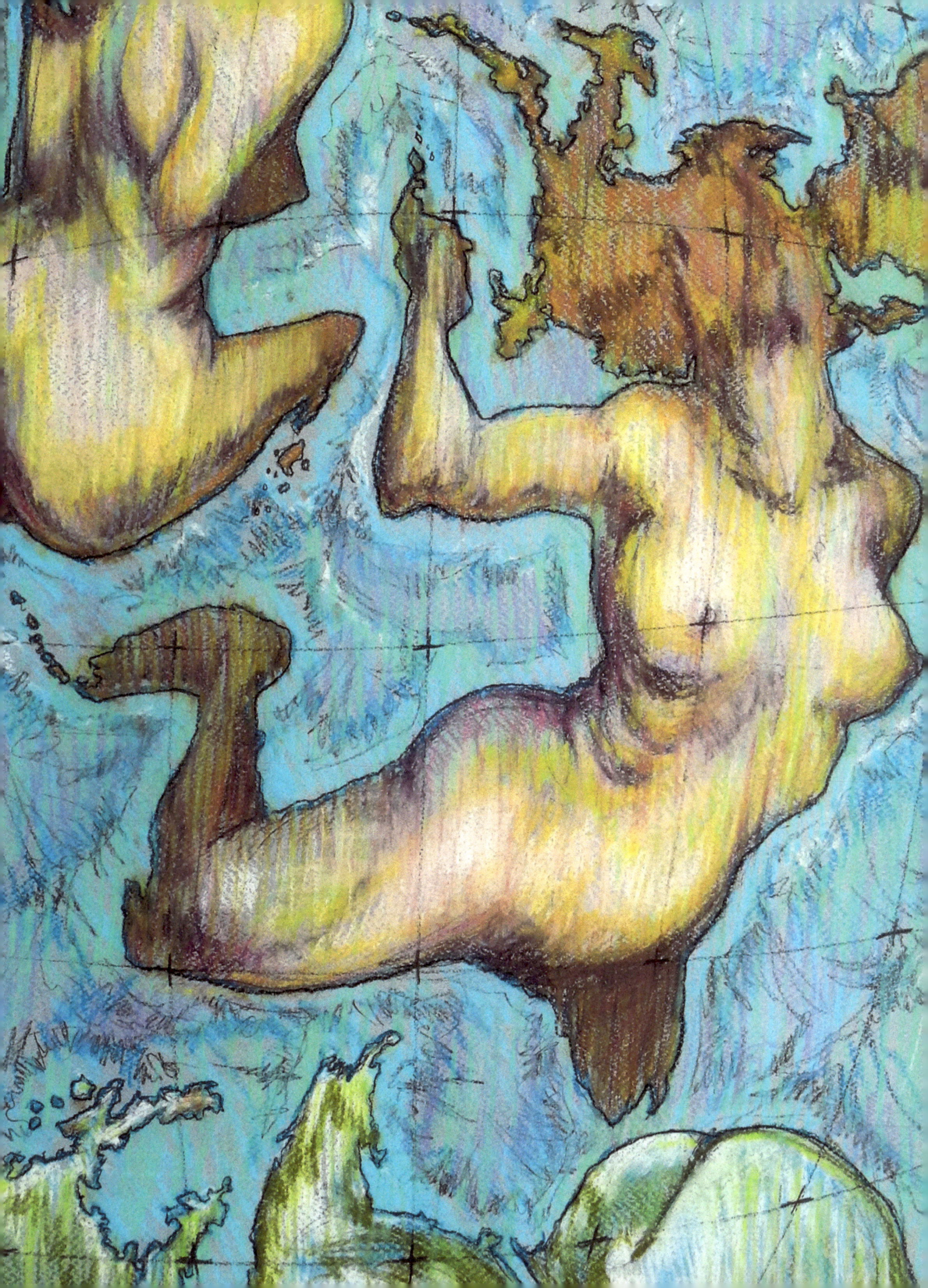

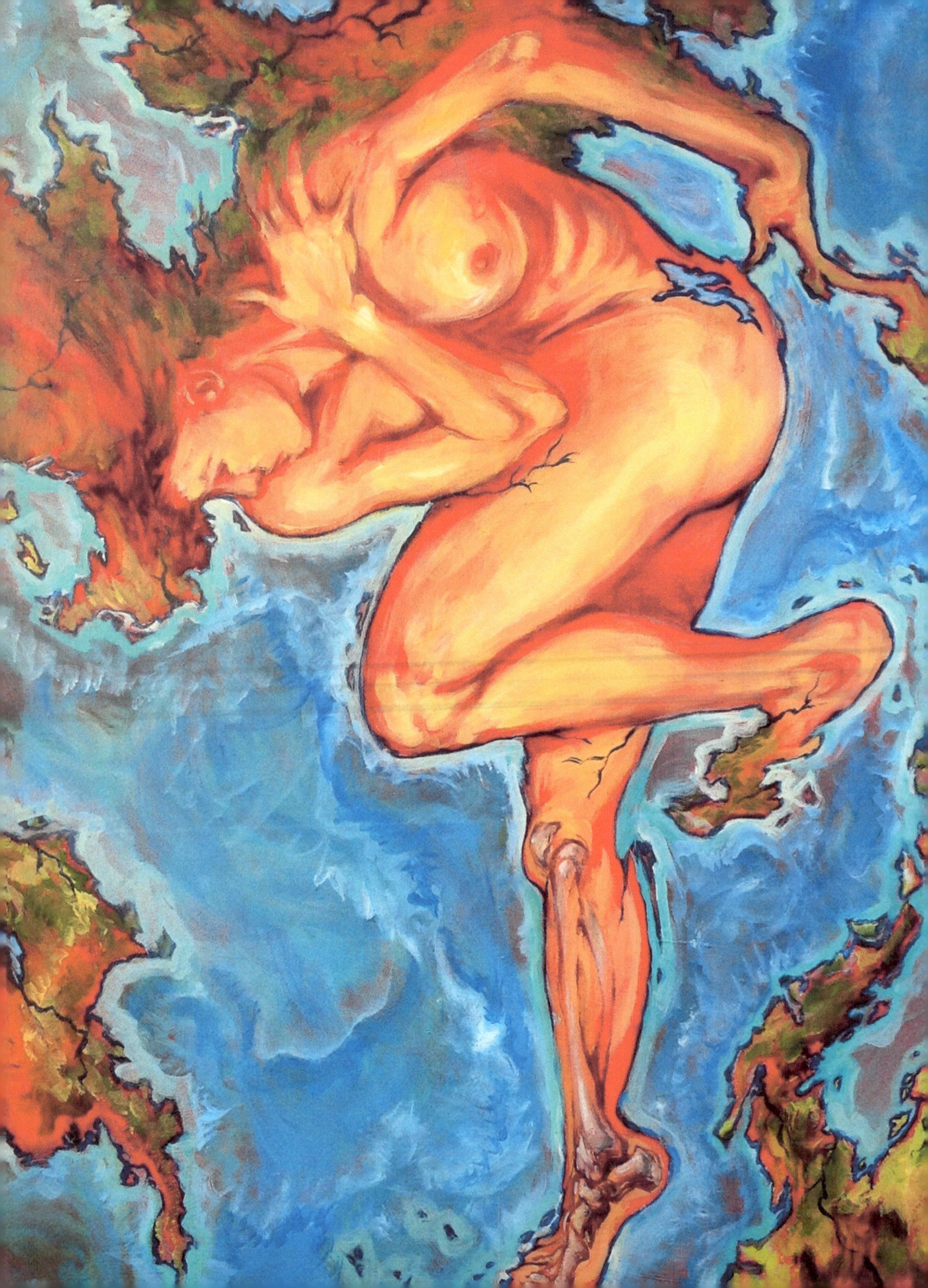

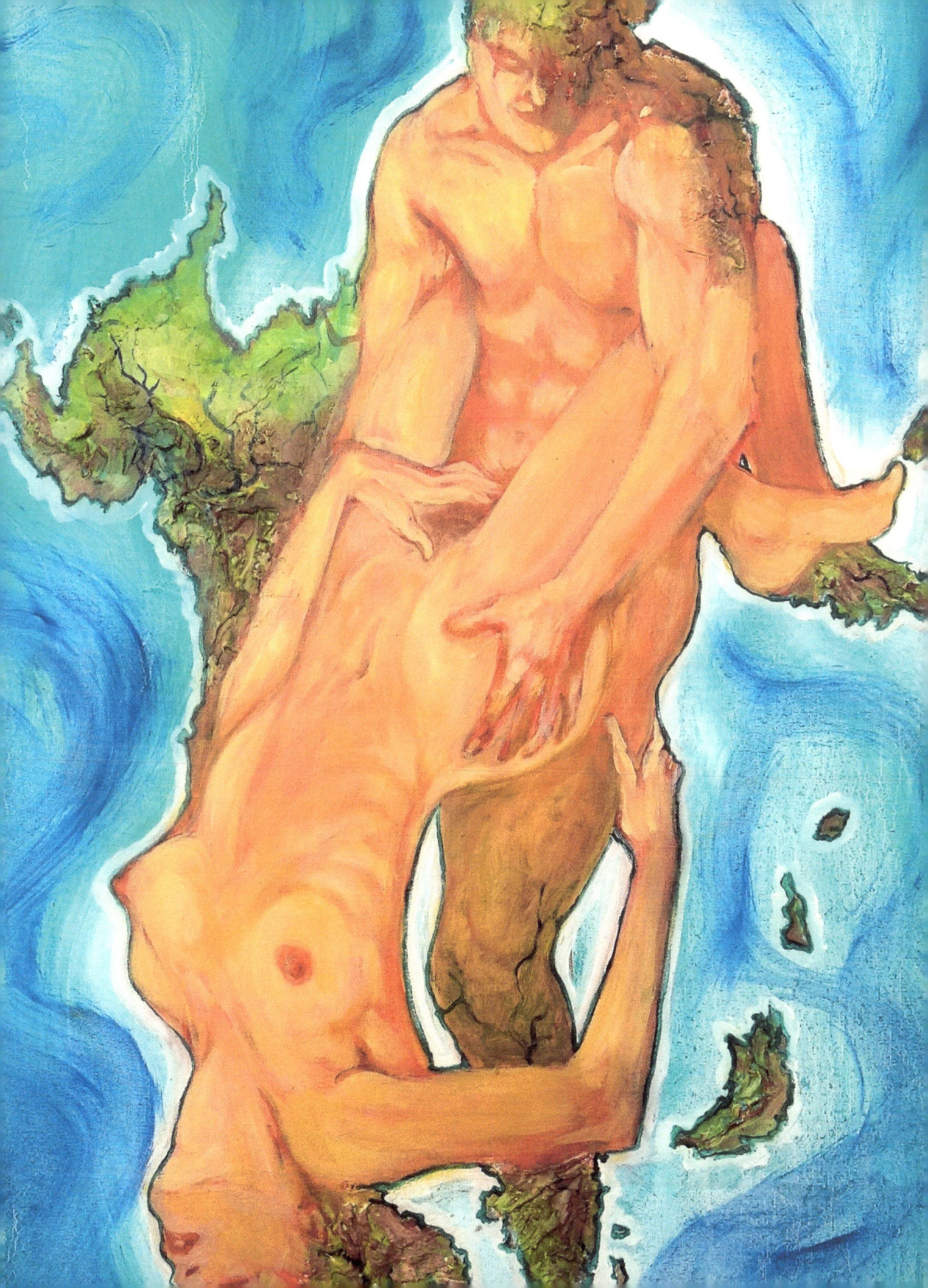

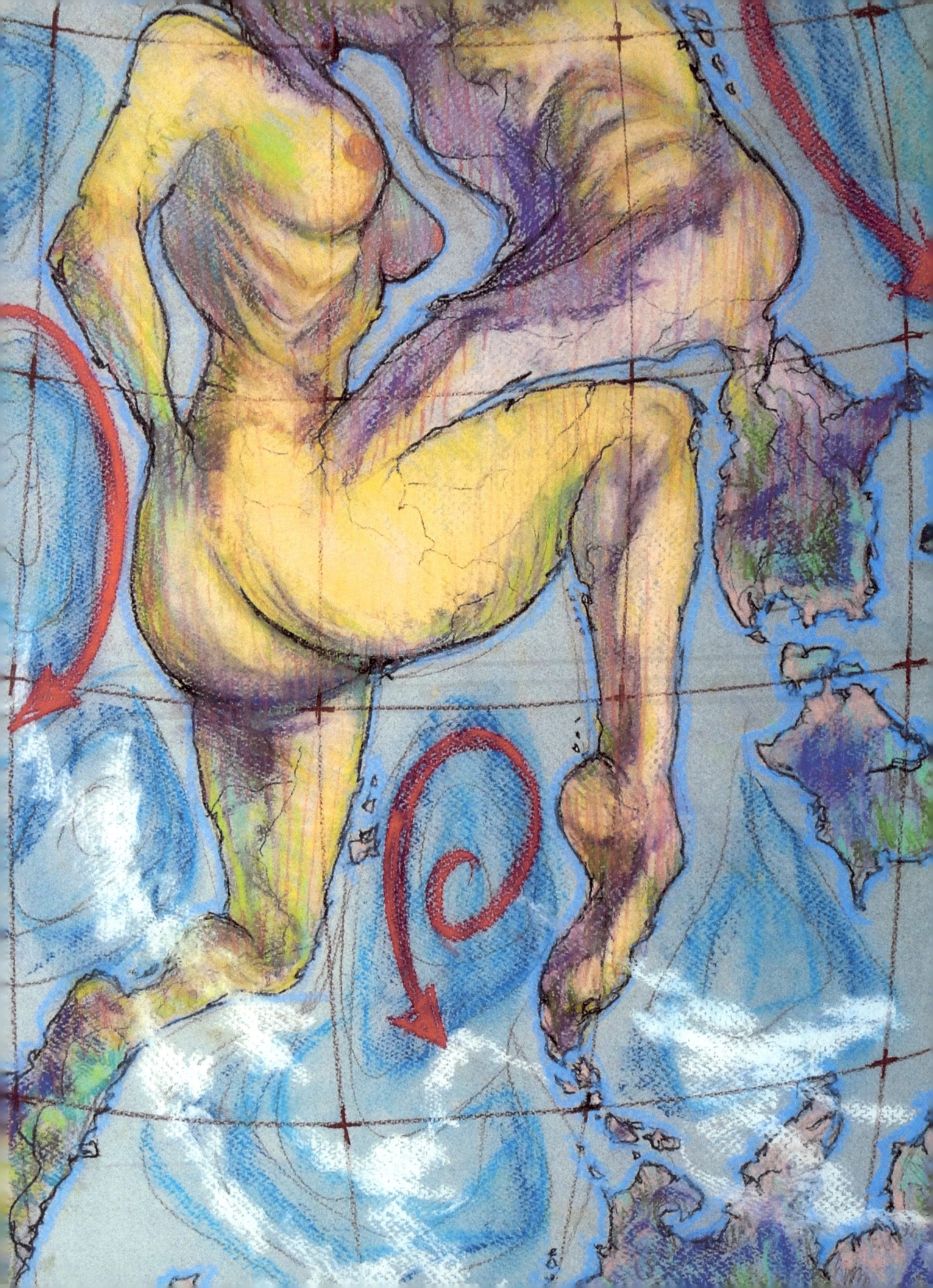

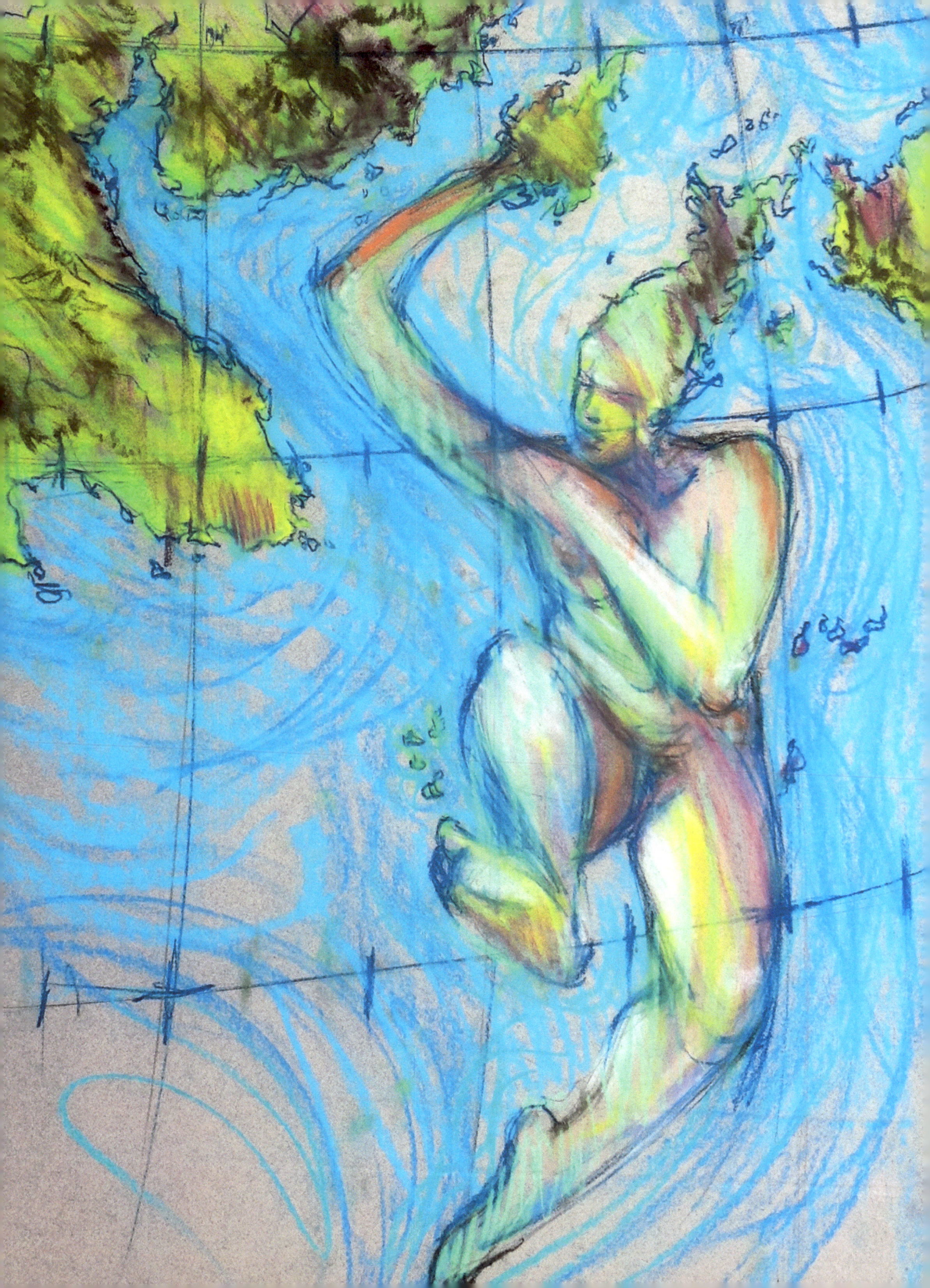

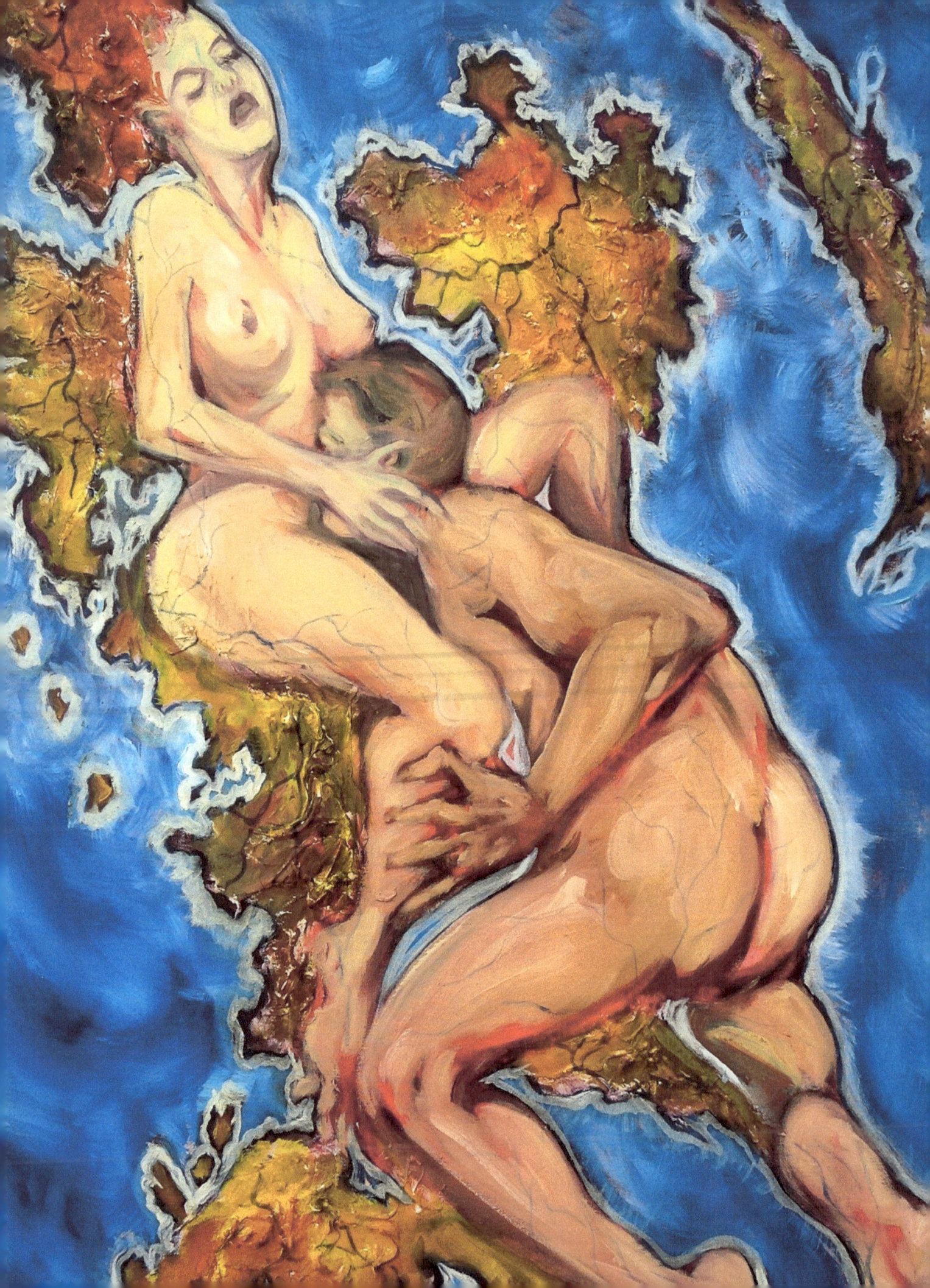

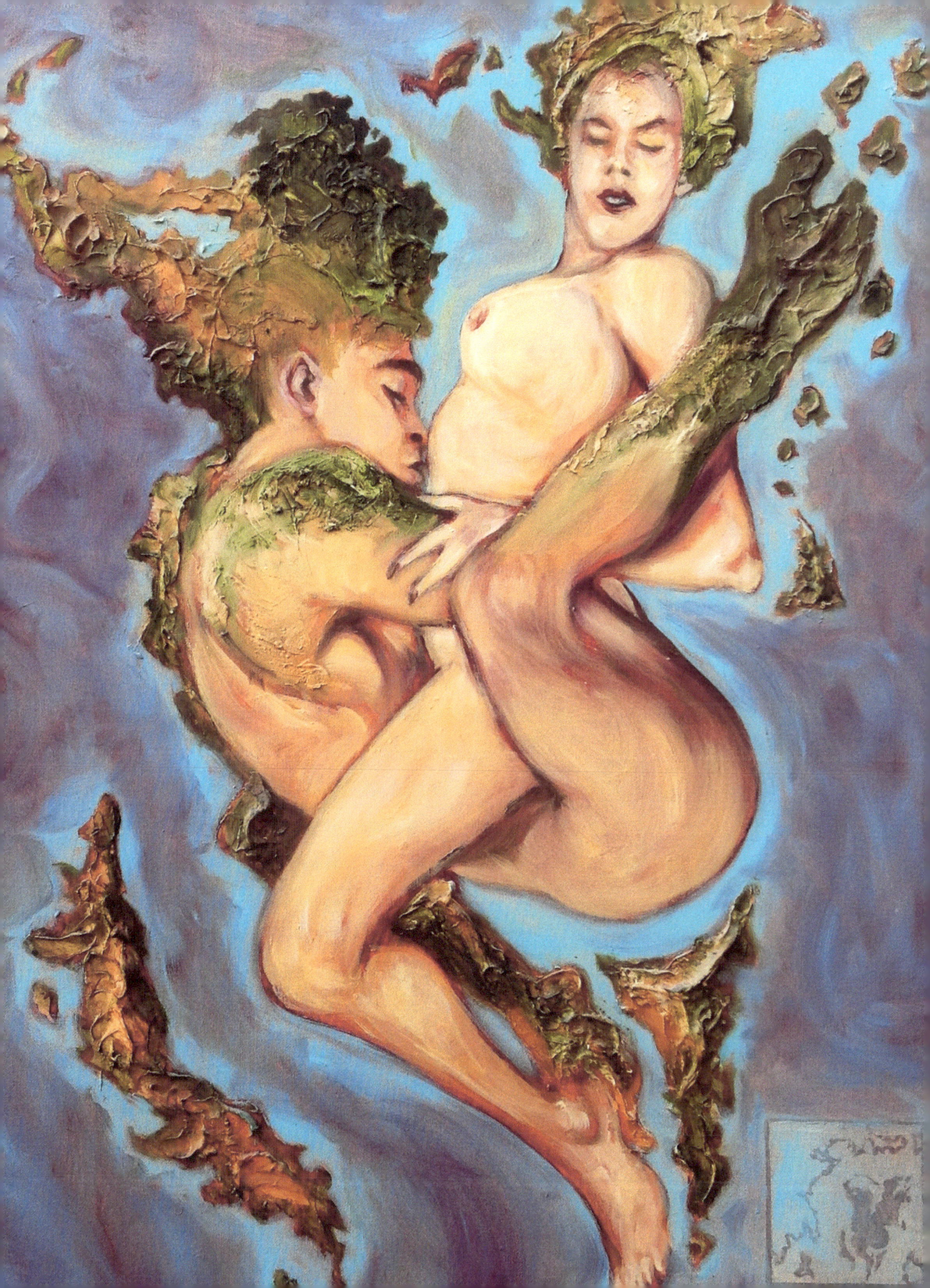

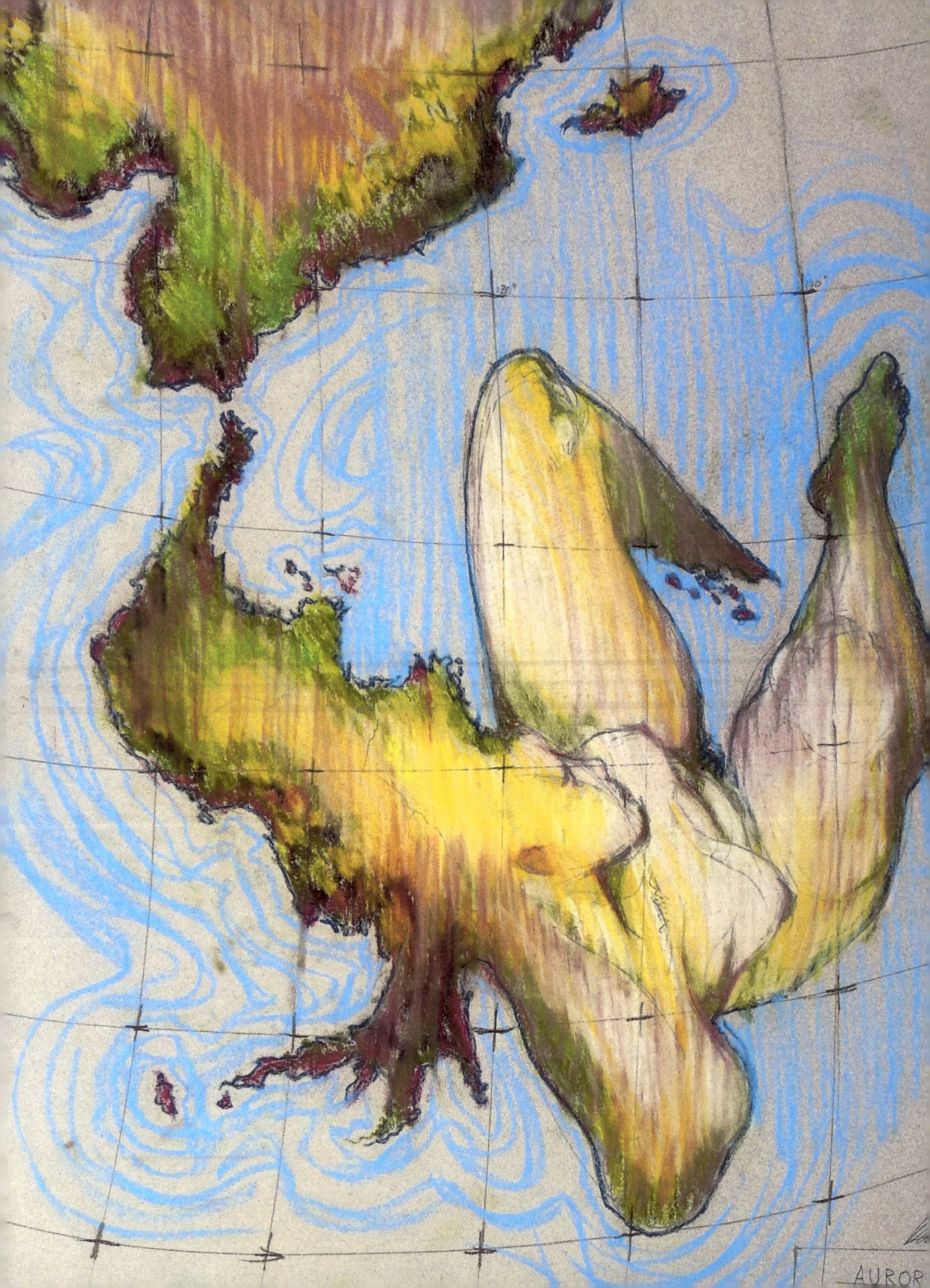

130°    140°

AUROR

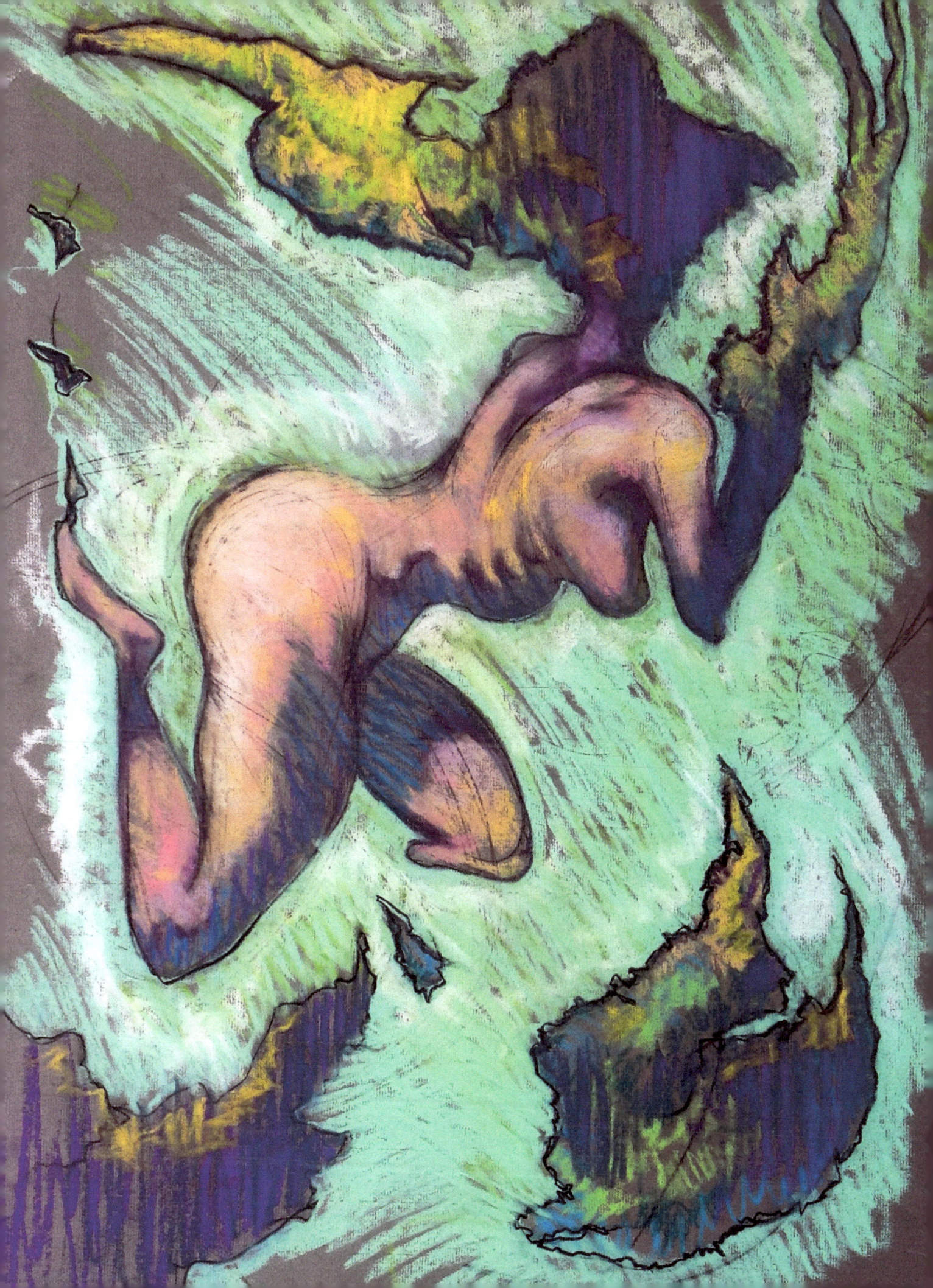

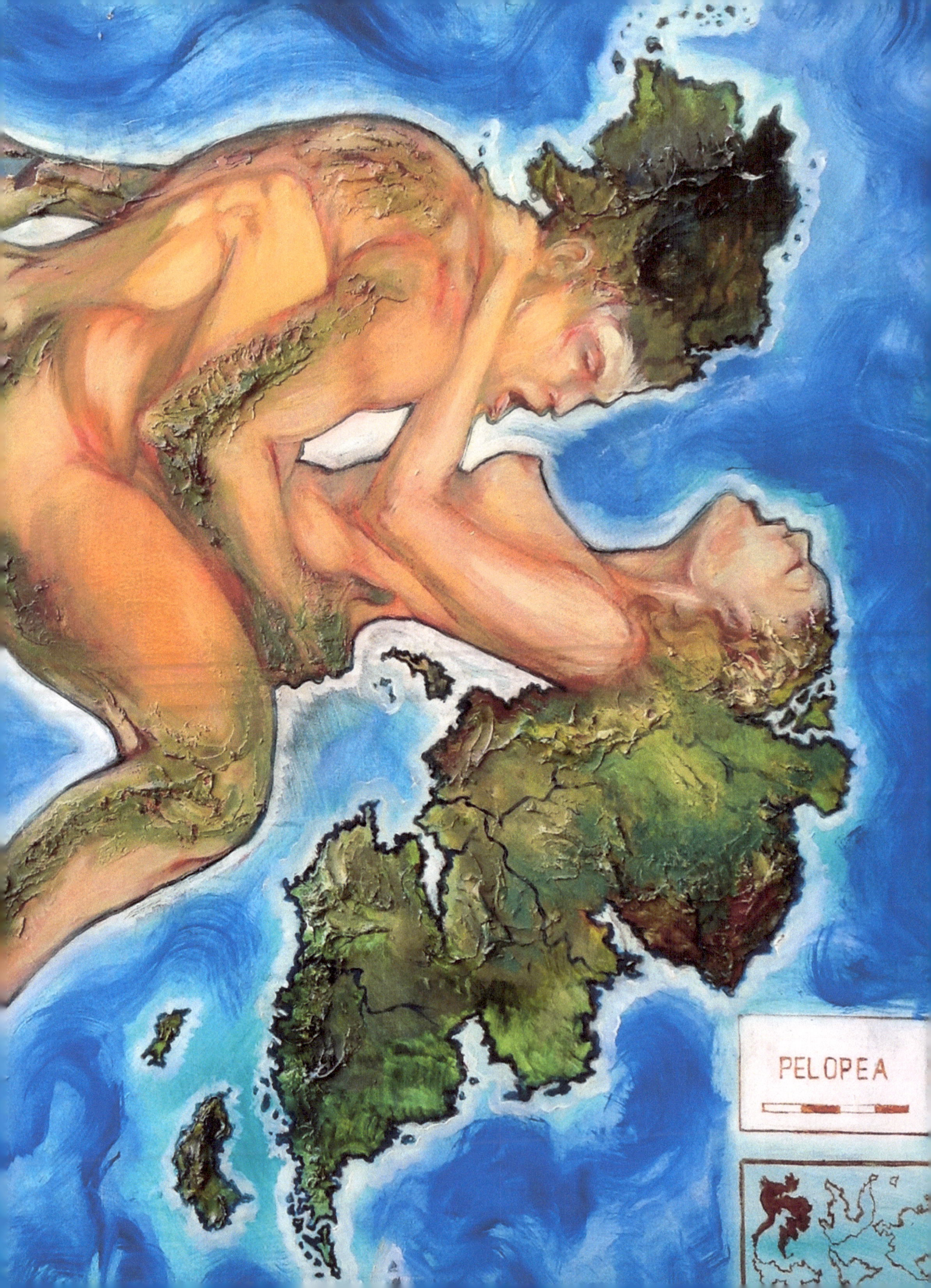

PELOPEA

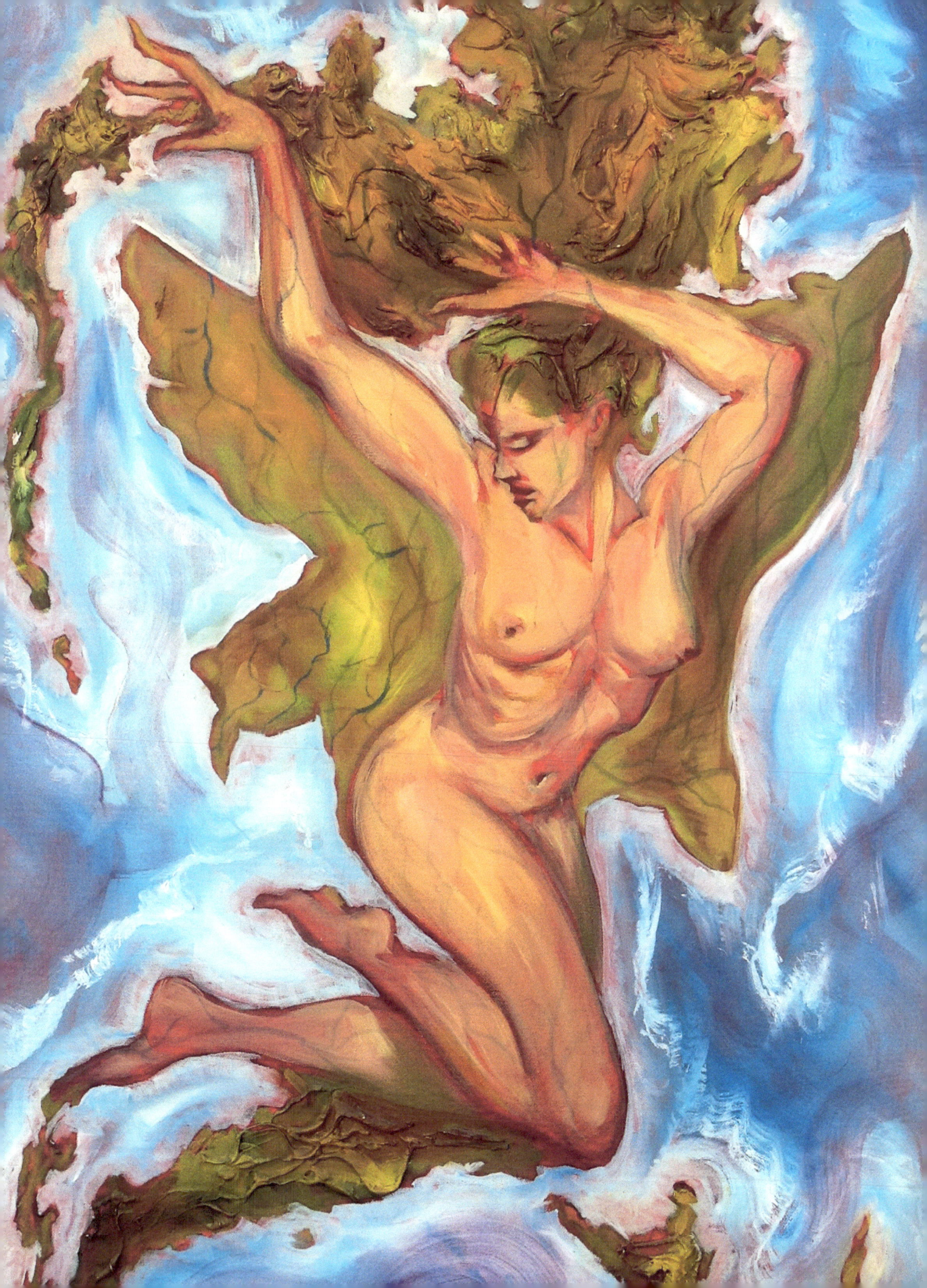

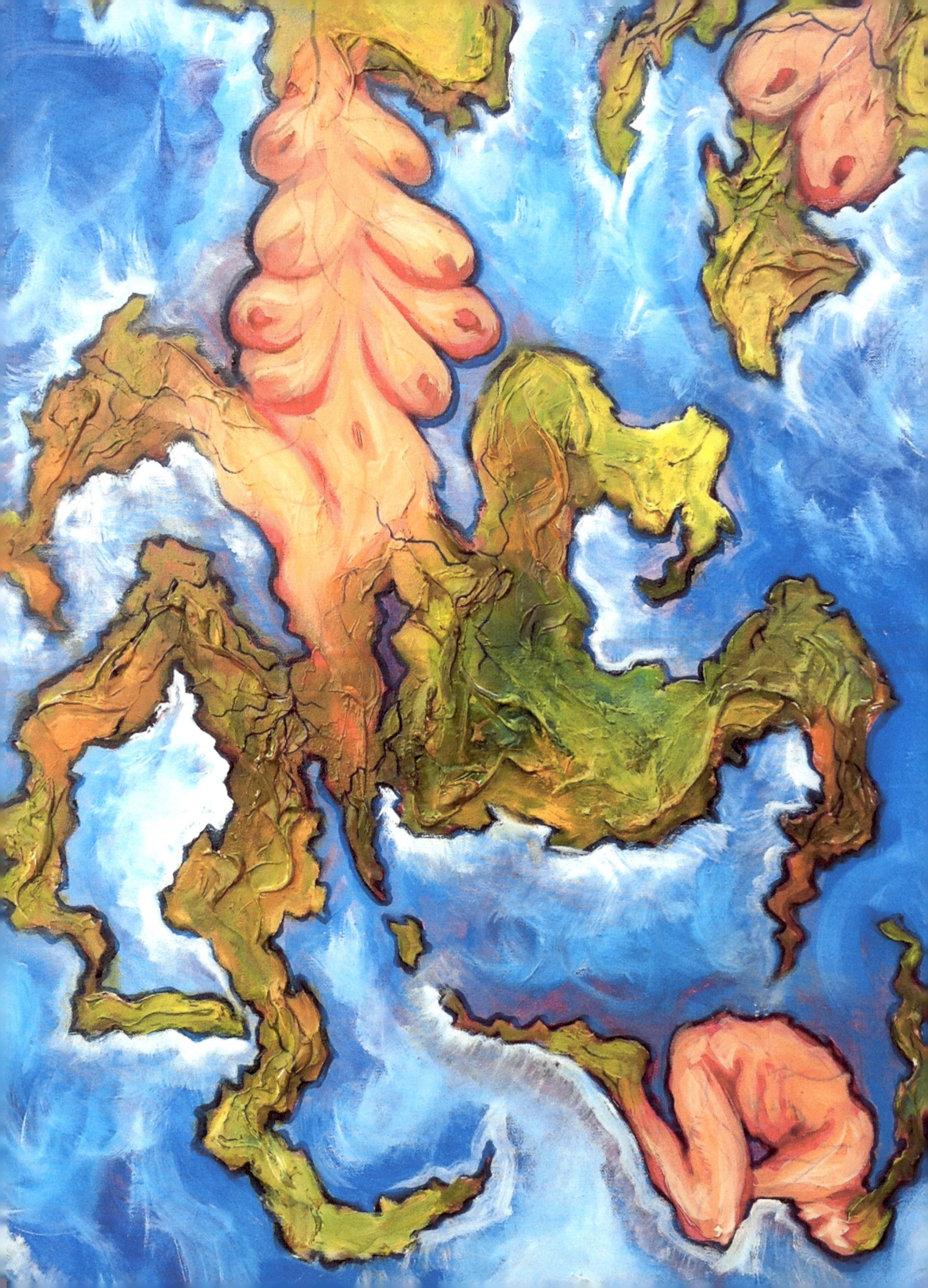

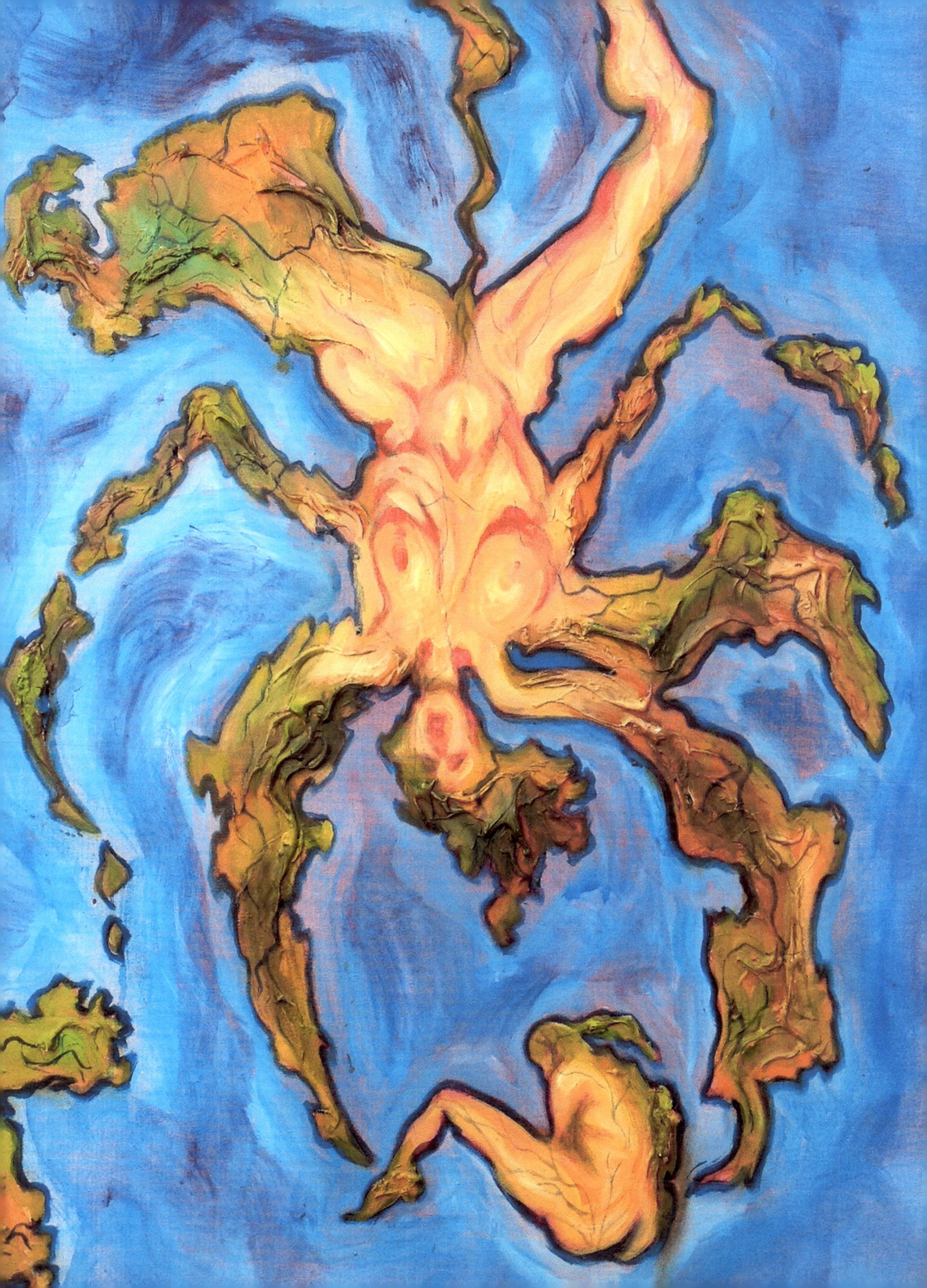

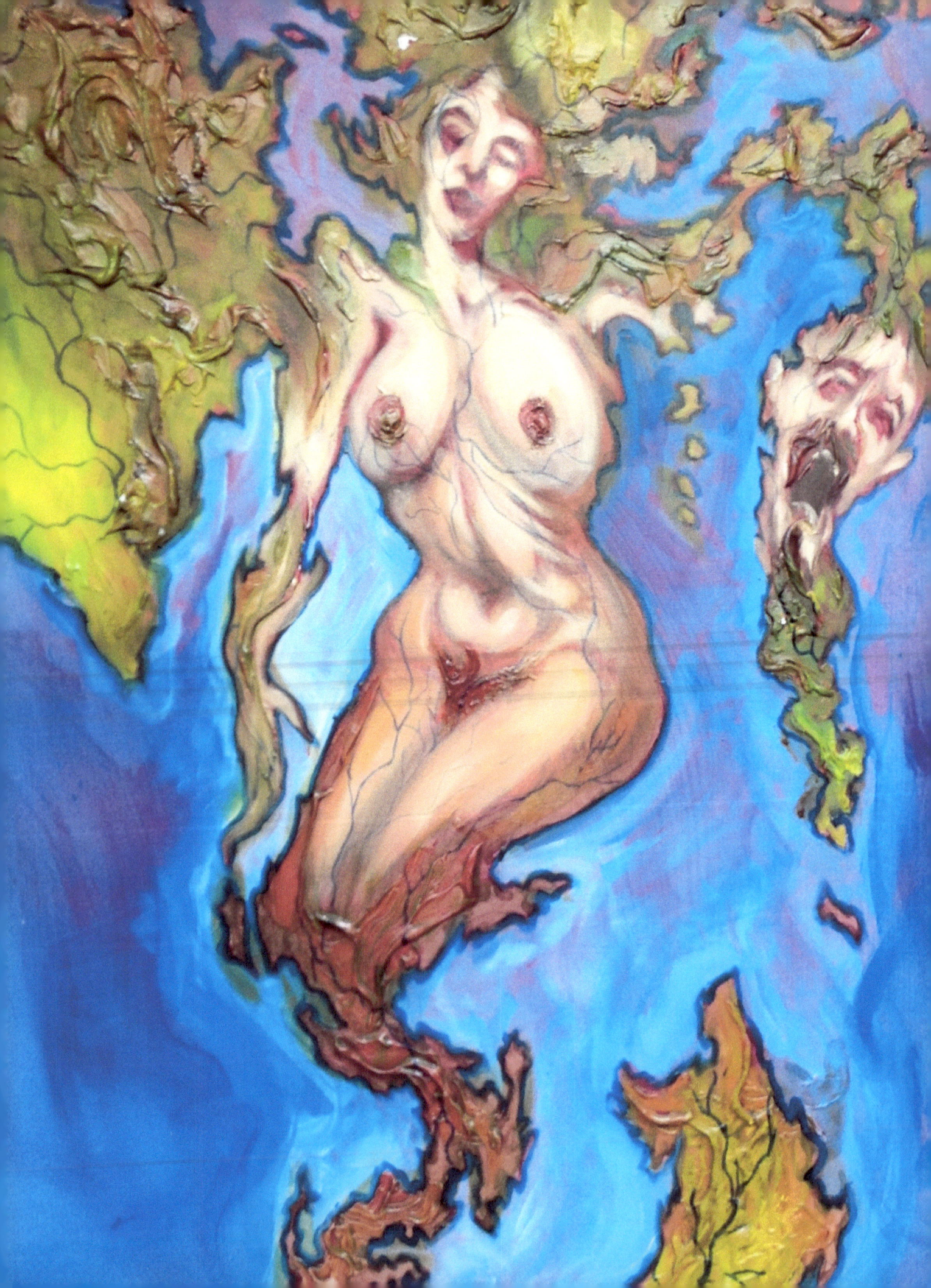

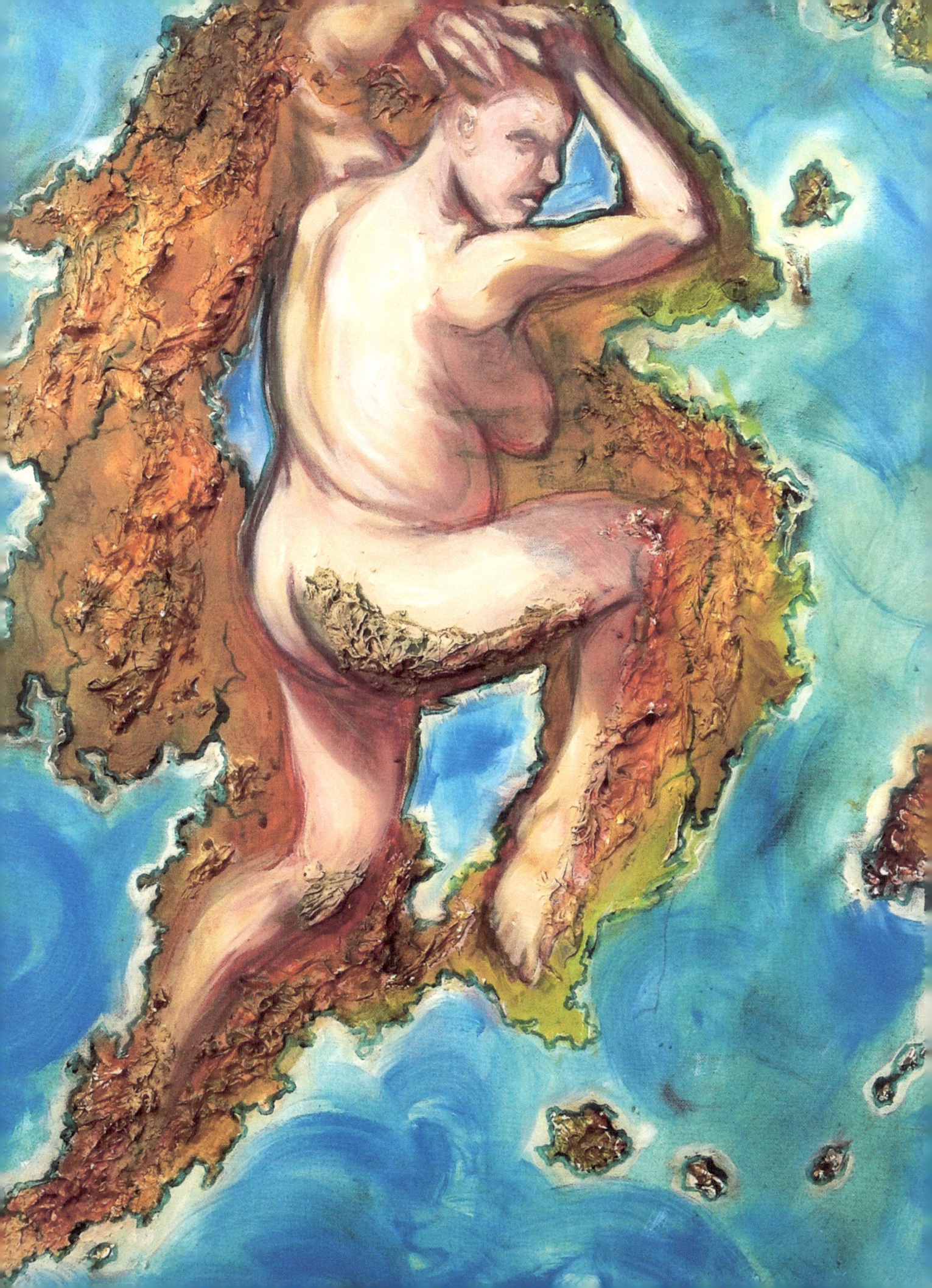

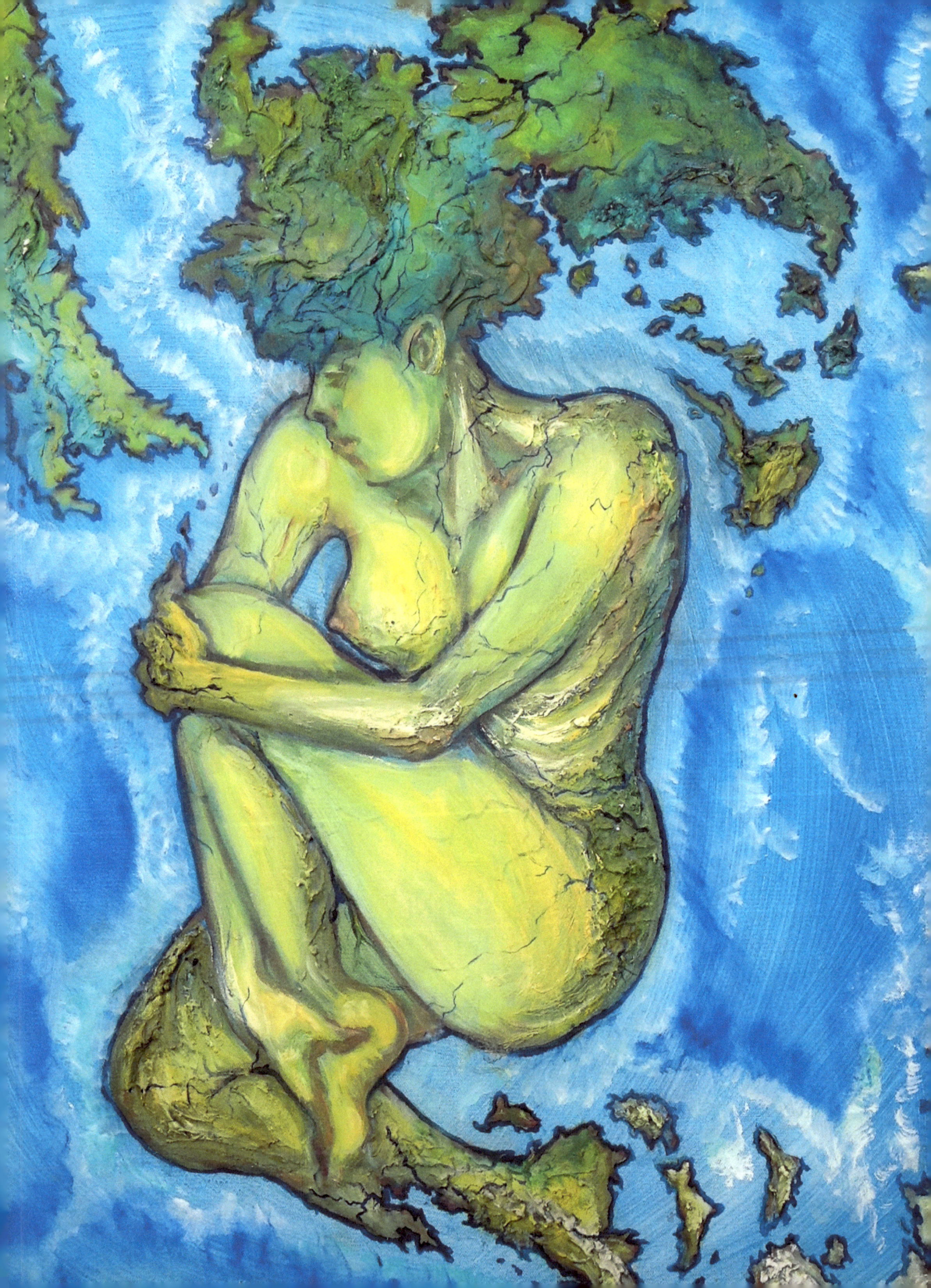

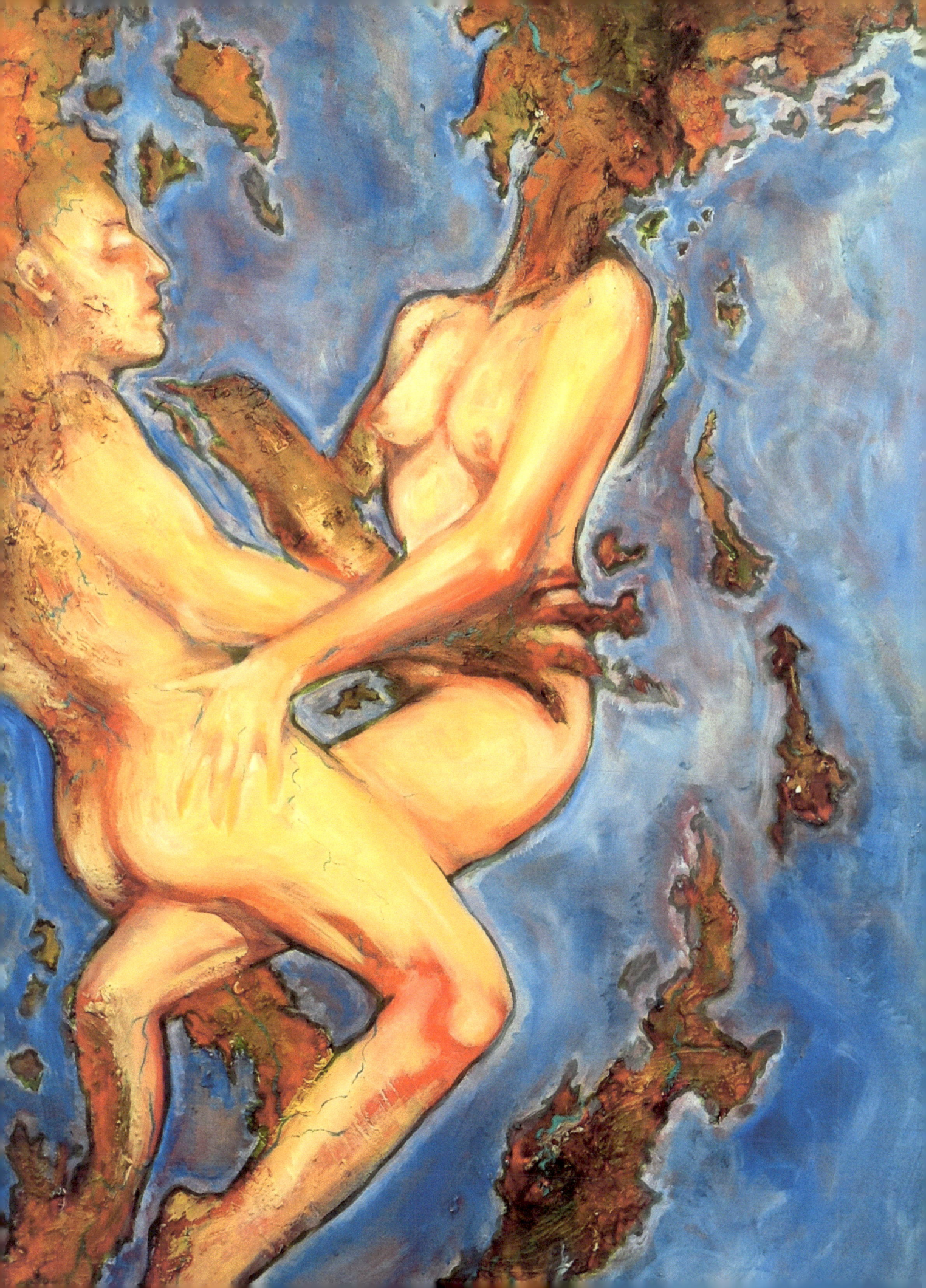

Special Thanks to: Martha de Perez Mitchell and
Robert Perez Jr., for the layout and their patience
in making this book into a reality.